"I NO LONGER"

A personal struggle with degenerative disc disease

Alice Randall Cocca

Edited by
Marie Randall Chandler

iUniverse, Inc.
New York Lincoln Shanghai

"I NO LONGER DANCE"
A personal struggle with degenerative disc disease

All Rights Reserved © 2004 by Marie Randall Chandler

No part of this book may be reproduced or transmitted in any form or by any means, graphic, electronic, or mechanical, including photocopying, recording, taping, or by any information storage retrieval system, without the written permission of the publisher.

iUniverse, Inc.

For information address:
iUniverse, Inc.
2021 Pine Lake Road, Suite 100
Lincoln, NE 68512
www.iuniverse.com

ISBN: 0-595-32483-5 (pbk)
ISBN: 0-595-66601-9 (cloth)

Printed in the United States of America

"I NO LONGER DANCE"

I dedicate this book
to my
dear sweet twin sister,
Alice,
whose life suddenly ended on
November 2, 2003.

This is a collection of her journals.

Contents

Foreword... xiii
From the Heart... xv

1994 1

1995 27

1996 61

1998 89

1999 115

2000 135

2001 155

2002 195

Closing 223
Your Stairway To Heaven................................. 225
Cartwheels In The Sky 227

Thanks to my loving husband, David, for his
continued moral support and for his shoulder to cry on.

Thanks to my beautiful, loving sons, Austin and Marshall.
Thank you, Austin, for your knowledge as you
continually guided me through the preparation of this book.
Thank you, Marshall, for giving me the peace
and quiet I needed to write.

I give my deepest thanks and gratitude to my
mother, Elsie Randall, who gave of
herself unselfishly in order to help make a
better life for my twin sister.
Because of my mother, my sister
experienced the true meaning of love,
the closeness of a friendship, and the
everlasting act of kindness.
My mother manifested the perfect depiction of the
undying devotion and the ultimate compassion
that a mother has for a child.
My sister's life was continuously blessed because
of my mother.
"Thank you Mom for being there for
Alice and for being the best mother I have ever known".

Someone

Publish

My

Work

Because it needs to be heard.

Alice Randall Cocca
2000

Foreword

My twin sister was diagnosed with degenerative disc disease, D. D. D., in February of 1994. Almost 10 years later, on November 2, 2003, her life ended suddenly and unexpectedly due to complications of D. D. D.

My twin sister had to endure constant physical pain. D. D. D. is a disease that slowly degenerates your spine. At the time of my sister's death her spine was WORSE than that of a seventy or eighty year old with the same disease. My sister was only forty years old when she died.

Before this painful and crippling disease restricted her mobility, she was a superb athlete, excelling in swimming, gymnastics, diving, and dancing. She won medals in the Junior Diving Olympics, completed triathlons, and won many honors in swimming competitions. A gymnastics and swimming instructor for many years, athletics were a vital part of her life.

Writing and music were her passions. She was a published writer in the literary arts magazine, Gulf Breeze, of the Gulf Coast Intercollegiate Conference. She kept many journals during her illness and "I No Longer Dance" is a collection of the journals she wrote depicting her daily struggle of living and coping with degenerative disc disease.

This book is my gift to her; the book she always wanted to publish but never could due to her debilitating illness.

"Here is your book Alice! I love you".

From the Heart

As I read the words
You put down on paper
I know your heart guided your pen.

Flawlessly you composed
As your body lay wretched in pain.

No rough drafts
Your words were final.
They needed no editing.

Your gift of writing
Has now become your gift to me.
I cherish the pages of your life.
The memories you have given me to read.
Your voice speaks on the paper
You have left behind.

I cry.
I weep.
Your book of life is not make-believe.
Your story is of your pain and suffering
Inside and out.

"I NO LONGER DANCE"

As I turn the pages
My sorrow deepens
I too feel the pain
You once lived.
Your words enter my soul.
The gift you have given me.

Marie Randall Chandler

1994

So here I am
crying
dying in pain
D.D.D. really got me.
a cab driver once told me,
"A soul landed in the wrong body"
That's okay
cuz I'm waiting, hangin' on

TIGER

what must be done
upon a rising sun
we see you all alone
the illness you have shown

a rainy, cloudy day
dismal
in your graces
you lay
buried in death's wasteland

the comfort you gave
always there everyday
death such an ill
part of life

we were there
right beside.

a collaboration
another mess
to tear up
another part
of my daily scenery

rather rely on dreamery
this I do so well
see you in so well
a state of sleep
so dear to me

tears stretch
instead of my legs
shattered and broken
fire in their souls

cause for a fire
in my blood

tears I've cried
the fire inside
never dies
the phone man
never lies?

feel the coldness sweat
sweet upon my feet
a battle to forge ahead
every car goes by
they never
see the reason why
I sit.

does it really matter
anymore
can't keep any kind
of schedule
up and excited
at 2:00 AM
but really, for me
does it really matter
anymore?

D. D. D.

here we go again
another week
another thousand
to keep me out
of pain

go on and laugh
sarcasm
never got anyone very far
the heat's on too strong
no one here but me
and that hurts.

I know if he (whenever he) may be
here with me
he could do it
Tears roll down
my face of change
because without pain
I would not be this same.

Didn't know this DISEASE could cost so much

guess God had His way
when He created us
on our birthdays

on and on we go
with Lithium and doctors galore
can't ever rid me
of this disease

I'll cope
I'll live
in happiness
in tears

in manic depression.

a waste of time
to gaze into your suicide
smile, go ahead
while you wreck my day
seeing you
I hope you
   Do
    Die
     to
      the
       spirit
        of
        Scylla.

Really Need My Lithium

Through my looking glass
See a mirrored life
Feel the past of pain
Feel today's joy

Hardwood floors
What a filthy rug
Got to have daily drugs
To get through
Oh can't you see

It's not a choice anymore
It's a decision I made
Sobriety holds me
Oh can't you see I'm real
Please don't walk on me

Hardwood floors
Breezes blow thru the door

blue sky

rain down

change it

you say you know how

but it bleeds

wrings

and it twists

crawl on my knees

but I can't get up

so much I'd like to do

Gotta get busy

What I really wanna do

is change

what I'm going through

the needles just don't work

leave it to the man

leave it to the boss

so tired of all the extras

I had a pretty good plan going down

but since you invaded me

it's all upside down

and we all know

I used to handle it that way

but I really wanna stop

taking the pills day after day.

Scylla

you want me to swim?

walk?

NOT.

why me, Scylla?

guess I worked my ass off

For IT, huh?

I just wonder

am I going to be

this way

all my life?

The Wave

I can feel them coming, electric, moving through entire lower body

then through neck and shoulders and arms. Pain intensifies

especially in left side of body—mainly left leg—the back.

Causes almost total loss of concentration.

Swelling, crying as pain worsens.

Usually (depending where I am—bedroom, usually)

it takes 30-45 minutes to get to kitchen to take MEDS.

Breathing during this time is heavy as I try to alleviate pain.

Bluntly, I breathe as if I were in beginning stages of labor during

childbirth. The crying continues. I curl up in a ball.

Emotional

I feel a deep sense of frustration due to ineffectiveness of cortisone treatments. Not really knowing their relief pattern (how long it takes for cortisone to work). I feel desperation and despair.

I feel a tremendous loss physically. Emotionally, I realize I must accept what has happened.

Days that are painful and discomforting I cry a lot because I am unable to do the physical activities I want to do. I have stopped many things I used to do due to my "condition." Through AA however, I have been able to deal with the loss of dancing and gymnastics. Dancing, I know today, I cannot do. Surprisingly enough, the desire has ceased.

Gymnastics relieves much of my body/muscle tension, so slowly and rarely, I stretch.

Basically, since February 13, 1994 my life has changed drastically. The big one that twirls in my head is this one facet of my life that I completely cannot change. My discs have degenerated and I cannot heal them.

This is the longest trip,

The longest ride

I've ever been on.

The tragedy with
this one
is

I NEVER

GET

OFF.

faceless
without expression
flat appearance
ZOMBIED
Without feeling
empty stare
glare

LIKE THE WEATHER
IS OUTSIDE
IS ME
inside.

dark, rainy, drizzle,
cloudy, damp, cold,
brisk, DENSE

JUST HERE
IN EXISTENCE.

My eyes—

    really are dry

    still, I cry.

My head

    must weigh 100 lbs.

GOD

so long

so uncomfortable

so many pain pills

and so much pain

so hard to shower

want to curl up

and die.

Yea,
well hey—

no longer part

of the regular

human race

SAY WHAT?

Move up?
NO
Move down?
NO
Walk around?
NO

All to do?

LAY DOWN

TOO HARD

TO

MOVE

= disintegration

RELIEF?

ONLY
THROUGH
THE
TEARS.

AND I'M TIRED OF THAT TOO.

can't walk

clock ticks too loud

don't wanna stand up

long enough

to shower

makeup/hair?

doesn't matter

anymore—

that sucks.

1995

NO REMOTE

so still
like snow
but this pearl's not shining
everything she writes
rhymes with dying

head so heavy
best foot forward
and I'd probably drown
'cuz I can't get up
once I lie down

Remember yesterday, Alice?

Remember the easy stride in your walks with Remy?

Remember doing gymnastics and feeling so good?

Remember going to WalMart and walking up and down?

Yea.

So TODAY—

Right side pain

I guess yesterday is the answer to today's "WHY."

TOO MANY

GOOD TIMES

brought me

the endless

lay DOWN

DR.'S OFFICE

how do you take this
lying down or upside down
a cup of tea
to assist your misery
a drop to fill
the empty pages between

scripts fills the bill
and hands examine me
walking a fine line of desperation
do away with the feelings
of anger and frustration

the only way to the lake
I believe we've got to take
sit down and have some cake
the only way to the other side
is thru the jungle baby

so I ask
sittin' down or standin' up
from behind I'd like
wait some more
to go back
behind my Dr.'s door

another night

waits for next day

sleep and more sleep

'cuz the bedroom's so cold.

SO HARD
to

**ACCEPT
MY SLOWING**

down
in this present life.

Almost the hardest
Because
this
is
lasting a long
time.

Thought it'd be over a day or two.
Huh?—like sore muscles. NOPE.

CENTRIFUGAL FORCE

jump inside and feel
feel inside of me
why I can't look
like others who see
jump inside and feel
feel inside of me

what tears do I cry
from the heaven's groan
twisted up and twirled
use my pelvic bones

the main thing
the ingredient missing
is people around me
they are foreign
do not even touch to understand

if only you could jump
jump inside and feel
and feel this pain
inside of me.

"Gotta go

Gotta hurry

Gotta go

go

go

Can't stand up too long."

lots of doctors to see
hopefully one
will reach into my misery

another real world
changing like the sky
but this time I can't fly
so I lay by the door
and feel the tears
I have to cry.

The Bitter Cloud of Pain

- unable to focus

- cannot carry through one simple task due to loss of conjunctive thought process

- like a whirlwind, patient becomes confused on "the next right thing to do" due to the increased swelling magnitude of pains

- remains in this CLOUD until patient able to take meds.

FOOTWORK

four times seven
used to fly in heaven
see me in the dance
lights glaze
over my magical hands

"The things I used to do Lord
I can't do them no more"
lay down
lay down on the floor
what once I held in gold, now
I lay down on the floor

remember the barefoot floors
cement and hardened wood
twirl around and around
jump up, swing down

lady in gold
diamonds and lace
leather and sweat
feels she'd be better off
dead

IS THIS EVER GONNA STOP?

I DON'T KNOW, EITHER

for days we could struggle
hours without end
we could go over this
again and again
we can lay it all out on the table
and still you're not ready
not capable
of taking a bath
of taking a shower

we go on and on
hang pictures up to carry on
blue lights and candle bulbs
still
you are not satisfied

so we deliberate
and you like to go on and on
you have reasons strong
sometimes not even sure
of the real reason
you're still not ready
still not capable

The dread
of the BATH?

Slow

Down
Now What?

Oh

if we

could

do it

ALL again

Blue
 ANGEL eyes

HEAR
 MY SPINE

CRY

SKY LIFT

season of pain

season of change

from the boots

from the jeans

from the red lipstick

loud rock-n-roll

and black leather jacket

time to feel

the bones inside

the muscles' cry

rubbing my eyes

searching for light

Walk on Heels

crowded stage

fluorescent light

brought me back

to spinal chord

progression lessened

a slow and easy lesson?

tip toe my life away

where I once held

crowded stage

flow scent

life in light

brings me to

a new season in my life.

Affect Me...How?

1) unable to feel good

2) angry because cortisone not a lasting solution

3) feel unattractive
   - no longer the beauty I once was
   - bottom of physical appearance
   desire getting dressed is no longer
   the JOY it once was—now painful, aggravating, frustrating
   - before my dress symbolized the excitement and passion possessed with flamboyance—eclectic clothing, jewelry, colors because I was VERY HAPPY!!
   now—just "SO, SO"

4) feel DEBILITATED—mainly my MUSIC—where is it?
   don't want to listen anymore—don't feel good

1) due to DDD…Pain, discomfort

2) DDD   1) hard to stand up
                  or sit down and do hair because arms are up
             2) hard to put legs in jeans,
                  tuck things in

3) EMOTIONAL LOSS—due to severity of physical pain, my passion
                        for life is disintegrating!
                        No longer desire music except for a few,
                        infrequent times of day.
                        because of mental loss—give up

Resentment List

1) inability to casually move around

2) long period of pain

3) physically hard to: 1. fix hair

                                  2. get nicely dressed with jewelry

                                  3. put makeup on

4) emotional loss—devastating emotional loss

5) do not have passion for music and running around town

STARING AT THE CEILING

a tidal wave of tears
red swollen eyes
so tired of the fight
she tries again
to rise from bed
hoping today
will bring the friend

it's not easy
the remembrance of yesterday
remains
she pulls the covers tighter
and curls into the pillows

only hope remains
that someday
the pain is going to go away
only hope will save
the faith for a better day
because she remembers
what it was like
yesterday.

the active
has grown so passive
"the things I used to do
Lord, I can't do no more"

what it is
is a struggle
to face my pain
to remember the enlightened days
now have really
turned around

sit in and gaze outside
only to fly at night
my spirit's in the sky
still in line
with the stars

SUNDAY'S PAIN

bones of steel
blood veins of cement
soiled chords
wrapped in black
stiff and frozen
no ice to break

the tears well
wishing for waterfalls
icicles drenched in pain
no sunlight
to bring the rain

locked in
cannot move
curled in pain
legs up on the bed

the knowledge to know
the pills are in another room
she can't go
because the pain only grows
and it's all been a circus
of people, pills and pain
never knew
and she never thought
the dance would end
the crash set in
and the ride she's on now
feels like it's never going
to end.

Sunday's PAIN—do you remember Sunday's pain

don't even want to try
afraid of tomorrow
and the pain that comes
not enough pills
'cuz they really can't
do the job anymore
then I remember
the blue shoes
walking out the door

what a sight
to see me try
neighbors probably hear
my painful cry
doesn't really matter anymore
I give up
because the process
seems to have failed
ain't no guarantees
for his needles to bring relief
one more option
one more try
I'm gonna give it a shot
tomorrow at 3 o'clock
               …Wishing IT would all just go away.

no red leather
no snake-skin
funny it works
how they look

ORTHOPEDIC
SHOES

Roll Away

better than
I thought
it would be

freedom in flight
wheelchair's more
than my appetite

if you think I got looks
      THEN
you should see me
      NOW!

No More TV

got a big, bright world to see
with a broken bass box
doesn't really suit me
but I'm out of the house
no more TV
no more TV

special parking for me
the rest fly in the trees
yea, and you can yell at me
doesn't matter
'cuz I made it to Sixth Street
no more TV
no more TV
people twist my taste buds
can't dance
but I know that's my floor
eyes up and head for more
soon be knockin'
on my Doctor's door
couldn't ask for more
all in it for me
no more TV
no more TV.

THE STAY AT HOME

found a free world
with all walks of life
took a while
to finally arrive
made it
now the day's to survive
come in like a storm
way up the scale I go
can't walk
can't talk
only lie there
with the TV remote

it's a day I wish not to commend
it's the way I live when the pain sets in
soon be over
soon be over
sleepless nights
nothing to do
am I losing my soul?
when my life
lies with the TV remote
my free world
my stay at home.

NO FUSS

I picture in my head
the moves
so smooth
the moves
only I can create
take the music
the real way
nothing fake
it's something I miss
still no one can caress
the passion
quite like me

having such a good time
let the guards down
by the door man
he gives me my change
then leads me back stage
been a while for these days
as different as they are

still in my mind
SOMETIMES
I remain
a Hollywood star.

THE

RIDE

goes

all the way....

WHEELCHAIR

grace.

1996

my life feels like a circus;
the walker on the trapeze;
some days so sturdy and strong
nothing to combat my worldly rein
stone cold sober
with nobody to fight

other days I am the sleeper
the loather living in sloth
anything else seems completely insane
God! I hate those days
no hope and cent

FEAR OF MY STIFFNESS

…feel very stiff

…rather do nothing than experience the discomfort of walking, bathing, hair/makeup, dressing. Desire is there but physical discomfort usually wins and keeps me inside too often.

THE TOP OF MY LADDER

Patience

gotta

CLIMB

first

ONE DAY AT A TIME

BLACK BACK

rounding the corner
to old age and pain
return the butterfly
embossed in grace

the road is short
some days so long
groping in the darkness
I pray for healing

cover ups do me fine
always low in supply
extra weight I carry
the disease takes me
somehow still carry on

laughter and spinal smiles
I embrace
learning to live in pain.

DUG DEEP DOWN

inside the drop of water
she crawls to escape
something so fluid
surely I can use
maybe a lighted fuse

pearl inside there
so hard for you to survive
let the crowded chaos
of the world around
take you deep, deep down

centipede legs
crawl, they try anyway
easier to stay in my shell
how long it's taken
how you've shaken

such a different life
all I ever see is white
(praise God for that)

RUSH 22

slow trigger to freedom
lots of knees bending
up to the sky
we can cry
later,
we die

push the food aside
mirror instead
God finally—meds
out on the homestead
better be me
rather than the TV

shuffle out to the streets
lonely feet make it easy
to lose the beat
make it faraway

BUT PAIN?

it floods
it agitates
it hits hard
against the shores
of my life

leaving behind
its nasty scars.

"I NO LONGER DANCE"

blue to soothe

blue to soothe

bones gotta move

easy on the vote

hand on the remote

"such a different life"

got it made

with my whites

not the end of my rope

straight dope

morning again

mourning again

SHAME PAIN

it's a shame today

illness came her way

talk too much

ingest the fumes

taught a new day

had to with her doctors

staying away

what a shame today.

CIRCLING

    IN

        THE

            TRAPEZE

                OF

                    DOCTORS.

That's how I dance now.

HEAD SPIN

strangled again

getting rid

of the head spin

new meds

put me to bed

better off

with the quit

and so I will

get a real

head spin.

SUN MOONRISE

cold water
rush through my hair
revitalize
this heat-drenched body
of summer's laden heat

seems funny
my course took a major turn
no more sun on my face
tanning winter white skin
brings illness to me now

a new venture develops
inside AC, with AC
cool the brain
rushing shower exhilarates
the hot sun burn

return inside
to my world of art
hear the music
of a new life found.

THE EMOTIONAL OVERHAUL OF PAIN

guess that's why
so tired after the chains
day.

ONLY WAY TO GET

THROUGH
This
TROUBLE?

GOD.

And that's ALL.

what I'm going through
oh, if anybody really knew
exactly the compass
of what I'm going through

probably would have a long time ago

if you could feel
the severity of the tears
the agony of the walk
but you can't

The pain of the invisible knife

PAIN

What does it do?

It restricts

like a boa.

evade—
physical pain
a dozen bricks
on my back
wanna feel life
my way?

still no drink
not an empty glass around
sure would like
to dance this town
but all I can do
to feel good
is lay down.

what a bummer
what a ride
wanna live this life?

THE FIGHT INSIDE MY SPINE

I wanna go
wanna be there
wash my hair
run around the block
dance
twist and shout

stand erect
walk with elegance and grace
try as I may
staircases always feel the fall

presence of today
lingers through my fingers
until once again,
the bed.

A Rose in Winter

blue jeans
T-shirt
and sandals

a little bigger
a little more baggy
but the shoe fits
so I decide to buy

no malls
no circus arenas
no Neiman Marcus
no run around
only straight to the thrift store

can't fit the shoe I once wore
but I've got my world at home
better today than yesterday
got my pills
makes the pain go away
it's me. Summer. AC.

so fast
nothing held me back
out past dawn
hear the DJ
afternoon in my luxury
king-size bed

not a worry to care
next stage show
and what to wear
I was the star
in the red, red car

all my friends knew the sky was mine
from black to blue
never thought
there would come a day
when I couldn't move
The fastest slow down
I ever had to learn
Feel the fire burn, burn, burn
seems such
a frazzling sight to face
this new way of life
when head says "go"
and the body demands "no!"
I pushed and pulled
trying to make this go away
trouble with DDD
it always stays
and decides to stay…… .

The f—' pain makes me angry 'cuz I can't do what I want—vacuuming without a heart attack would be nice.

I've got more limitations to add to the list now with DDD and meds. My only moments of pleasure and joy are when I take my meds. They run out so so fast. What a f—' RAT RACE!!!
DDD has robbed me of my most prized passions of life: swimming when I want/MUSIC!!
My hair? Oh well. Traveling to see Christina is cumbersome now.
Can ya' believe it? No singing = No joy. No ambition.

I've laid on this couch with this horrible TV on more hours than I used to. But somehow God hears my prayers. The reason for lack of joy and ambition is DDD. It's taken over. Pain that operates on its own schedule, never adhering to what I might feel or would like to do.
Food became joy . . for awhile. THAT I can control with success. But pain—it floods—it agitates—it hits hard against the shores of my life
leaving behind its' nasty scars.

SWIM

could there be a way
to bring back yesterday
let the door close
lead on to tomorrow

God give me strength
to make it through
Yes you do
Yes you do

this time is again around
swim would drown
so tomorrow
to the pool
I will go.

Outside the Steamboat

it's truly
yours again
in and out
the front door
still yet to win
so hard
to get my wheels to spin
another Friday night
I suppose I'm all right
deep inside
I'll wait
in the hot dog line.

Cipher Me Legally

the work
abandoned
weeds are my hobby
treacherous
blind
to my constant attention

sparkling lights
cool, cool whites
sunflowers and roses
acoustic guitar
peacefully abide

in a day's work done
only with V and Soma
not anticipating the crash
although that will come

limits on what I can do
my weeds know
all there is to tell.

POLICE PROTECTION?
anywhere

DDD
you thief
you rob me everyday
can't live without me?
you say.

found a home
deep inside my skeletal system
you don't even know
not the bit aware
of what you've taken and taken
"what never belonged to you"

it's black
and it's white
no middle ground with you

circling in the trapeze
of doctors.
That's how I dance now.

To the Dr:

-feel shooting pain in right leg
directly followed by tingling sensation thru whole left leg

-right hip soreness
-difficulty walking
-superb relief from VIC & SOMA
-SOMA aids in freer movements—with ease
-VIC removes pain

BAD DAYS pain excruciating and cannot find any comfortable position

-standing up straight—I cannot stand up straight most of the time
SOMA gets me in position to take shower, bathe, wash face, brush teeth at sink, etc, and drive car.

-I deal with a lot of muscle spasms making it very difficult to do much of anything. The pain persists, sometimes more intense that others (after simple household chores—sweeping, vacuuming, laundry, etc.)

1998

BOA

The pain
That won't go away
The fire
That does not die

The tense tightness
leaves no air to breathe
escape via of pills
The things
That used to bring me down

so restricted
and close to home
so tightly woven
into a haven of pain
stay everyday
The door I don't want to open
coping with my reality
and hoping
it will one day go away.

S
T
A   e
G   n
N   i
A   p
N   s
T

V. C. D.

white
remember you
came into my life
you let me drown
in my own pool
white

use you now
to cover the print
look pretty good
when you danced
with me
in lights
white
always afraid
I'll never get enough white—
everyday white
couple times everyday
white
have to cry I feel like dying
need to 'cuz I'm always crying

last night the rain
Today, there's pain

RADIATING

PAIN

BLOOMING THE NAME

in the doors—

IT (the pain)

is a part of me—

a physical, mental, spiritual
part of ALICE.
She (it) always exists.
Always here.

While sitting here, in AA
The pain accompanies me.
The feeling I can accurately
identify.

Feels like I'm constantly
carrying someone
on my back.

SCYLLA'S REIN

almost paralyzed in my shoes
never quite sure
what activity to do

so I lay again
down
hoping I'll get up
close my eyes
and feel the quiet
of my blue, my dark

and others walk my way
even worse
from day-to-day
but for those unable to understand
because they have not experienced
I watch them
almost resenting their freedom

but my struggle
remains to be mine
the curiosity of time
fingers through the pages
as I close my thoughts
and proceed
my way home

NOW IT'S COLD OUT

Tightening thoughts
Restrain me
What happened to the passion
The life
I used to lead

Filled with antidotes
Designed to release
In their designation of pursuit
Leave me empty
And confused

The nausea
The tired mind
Sting ray in my shoulder
Broken bricks against my back
The struggle to walk
Do my bedtime balk

The loneliness of my world
I remember the little girl
Now she's lost
Out in the jungle somewhere
All comes down
Ticktock go around

BUSY SIGNAL—CALL WAITING

lost my oneness with you
feel the hot water
turn to blue
what do you do?
provide a way out
for me, from you

stiffening bones
unable to move
it's that bath
I use to soothe

aspiring
in my nightly candlelight
tomorrow you really move
Vicidon I use
to soothe

despite the others' contest
my race has been won
the chill of the air
is warmed by the sun

you walk me around the house
tip-toe
creeping like a mouse
even here,
in my own house
crippled bones
sit by the telephone.

the drastic changes in my life due to DDD

- physical abilities (loss of)

- psychological difficulties of acceptance and how to deal, to live with DDD and its effect on my whole being.

I REMEMBER

this pain
will go away…

if not the same,
of me, this has tamed
and I've never
been the same.

POWER LEGS

to choose
the red or the black
oh, those leather boots

the rocker in me
so suddenly subsides
over a period of time
but I remember
those red and black
leather boots.

shadows eyes
lies behind
my curtain at night

watch her dance
hear her sigh
it's been a while
for a midnight ride

yellow captured soul
"for whom the bell tolls"
silly, ugly fool
drowning
in your own
swimming pool

jump, arise and shout
turn the music up loud
dance in midnight clouds

the climbing ascension
grudging the days away
dissonance everyday
watching the day
by day

farther on
in her balcony dress
red heels
hair's a mess
drag thru the streets?

soothe me
kindle these degenerated discs
I wanna move

UPON ARRIVAL

more than
walking on hot coals
need a shoulder
to lean on
pick up my legs
feel like a colored peg
awning his way home

struck a match
someone did
struck me with an axe
tire tracks
all across my back

surge energy
surge soon in my day
may I temporarily wipe
this nauseous pain away

wish I could express
this whimsical fancy dress
show you
just who I'm all about

volcano about to erupt
hurricane winds to corrupt
sit right down
think about what it is
tonight

a bit of an empty space
no expression on my face
no rains here lately
this pain—I drive you all
insane.

YOU
ARE

**Carry
On**

BAGGAGE!

"can't get rid of you!"

"Flame—Glo"

clothes dry
out on the line
coffee on the burner
a life lesson to learn
it's renewal, I yearn

cats are fed
I arise from bed
scaling my hair
wringing my head
sometimes I might as well as
be pronounced dead

clothes twirl in the washer
as I leave it alone
called an old lover
on the phone
still, I'm still alone

it's the D.D.D. again
choking my only friend
whites will do me fine
see the Christmas twine

begging for her return
one more time.

it's always been down
a swimmer's drown
the fancy dressed clown
and his disguise
a painted colored frown

feel the pull
dragging my feet
loud, loud music
infiltrating beat

blackened fish
chicken dish
can't cook tonight
climbing, climbing
where is my life
drowning in my spine.

ROTISSERIE

head back
or to the side
to the other side
closing my eyes

head down
moving around
trying to complete
the painful feat
trying to get to sleep

head back
or to the side
to the other side
circling in defeat

body down on its side
turn with obstruction
to the stomach prize
to the left
on my side,
back to black back
quickly again
turn to my right side

such is the life
for those
with a degenerated spine.

the stick-crick in my neck
sallow skin
wrapping my muscle
on a tightrope walking
like a weak, cold front

You're always there
accompany me
is there another side
to the deliberate pain
you try to disguise

a purpose?
wrapped up in your darkness
a reason
for your constant frustration
a map
outlining the chapters of my life?

I ask you,
oh degenerate, blackened spine.

While I sit and do nothing.

DON'T OPEN THE DOOR ALL THE WAY

her kindness
stretches across the map
lets me cuddle
in her motherly lap

unexpected turns
dominate my life
take away the strife
but always
give me a price.

SPINE

If you could
Waste my time
You'd be so kind

If you could
Take my pain
You must be insane
TO TASTE IT LIKE I DO

VIDEO MECHANICS

an author's dream
a carnival's clown
silly scheme
a hot thriller's
Hollywood theme
remains in me
to produce, to be

less and less
walkin' that 6th street crowd
perhaps a life to bless
someone in need,
someone, besides me

candles turn tonight
no flaws here
for I am always home
a giant change
I must learn
feel the spinal burn.

I'VE ACCEPTED IT.

1999

Ain't never

Quite sure

Exactly

WHERE

TO

GO

Bed?

TIRED of that

HAIR

JEANS

BOOTS

ACTIVE

I gave up dancing, now the DDD still proceeds.

REALITY CHECK

the rose refused to bloom
hot sun crowds her room
Anyone aware?
anyone really care?

out of the sheets
to my box of pills
still, can't do
the things I really want
many people
crowd my way

at home
I'd rather stay.

SEE ME IN THE MIRROR

the dancing
the living in the wind
the clothes, the hair
can you bring it back again?

hope for no return
the painful days you bring
this is one illness
I wake up with everyday
never, has it gone away

some don't really believe
doesn't matter,
because they are unable to conceive
not only my physical loss
but the passion for life
the absolute fire and zest
I once had for living
is black, gone
because you remain
no need to try anymore

FAITH

1) in acceptance but still difficult

2) God doesn't give us things we cannot handle

3) everything "one day at a time" will be okay

4) just maybe my back will get better—
   doubt it

"Where there is doubt, may I bring faith."

Losses with DDD

ALL DUE TO: physical disability

- walking—dancing!
- swimming
- showering
- moving around
- driving
- dressing
- my jeans
- my boots
- my hair
- activity level
- ambition to experience Austin
- looking good
- long periods of time spent running around town
- music—my writing/listening

= depressed/beaten/changed woman

TAKE

ME

from my pain?

F—

MY

HAIR

I belong in a wheelchair.

NEVER'S END

the staggering
never really went away
shots from doctors
never really promised a full recovery
the surgical procedure
denied due to you, Scylla
still with me
still inside

to wish for the past
that flight, angelic flight
the journey I thought
would never end
now, it's you Scylla—
all day
everyday

staring eyes
motionless upon the sea
gaze in bewilderment
wishing for life
the way it used to be

you are Scylla
a goddess I know
no one accurately knows
the life I now hold
only Scylla knows
only Scylla knows

SCYLLA'S SIGH

no room to move
space the acre
glitter me fantastic
spoken on the floor
wizardry of magic

fly on, she says
yet clings to my soul
cannot go, I cannot go
Scylla, you make my life so slow

death box of letters
the ones who never sent
belief one day
they would come
fly on, she said
fly on
someday
"maybe someday, you'll see the other side"

ambiguously tormented
sacred skeleton
come out of your closet
barred and chained
day after day

show your true colors
ambiguously tormented
society rolls outside
limited world of insecurity
verify yourself

slippery shower floor
earth's only resource for you
water is at your feet.

Rebound

less
of a person
no sky
no spirit
empty inside
with the TV
running all night

thought I could swing
the pills my way
so much security
having them here

now it's like Lithium
daily by doctor's orders
in it's darkness
I hid everyday
with curtains tightly drawn
while I drown

my last fall
this was God's call
the pain was unbearable
bruises, scratches, sores
from who knows where

This is the life in the life of a manic

Moon Cocca

I must find it
feel it
and the courage
no bandages
only I can change
this sadness of mine

how much time
all the same kind
reaching for the sky

waiting to fly
to fly to my moon.

SEE IT ALL

the pictures
tell a story
of who I was
where I went
who I was with

some say take it all down
my life—drastic handicap
I choose to invade
these walls
with anything

who means much.

One Morn (MOURN)

in the darkness
somehow brightens
in the light
I find

this life that's changed
the constant, chronic pain
home everywhere
legs like cement

is this
I have
perhaps somehow
I'll awake
in the light
and have a healed spine.

who am I
anymore
keep the door closed
some never understand
that's their weakness

for the last 5 years
for the last 5 years
on and on and on and on
on and on and on
this knife penetrates

tablets like candy
let me do so much
run out so fast
never enough to last

beyond there is light
to take me away
I think of it often
suicide
suicide

well, maybe someday

the Art of Alice
drawn from various sources
the shower awaits
like the pain
Came again
for a steady 5 years

my microphone
the rock-and-roll man
dressing for a shaking mirror
in need of so much
The Art of Alice
has done lost
her source.

2000

Another death

more dying

like the time

I crawl

on my hands and knees

Turbulence

a puzzle
the pieces all lay out
a choice to retrieve
or receive

can be a jungle
twisted turns
twigs trip
unable to see
just where
I'm going to

put it together?
God only the power
I jump to the shower
wash anxiety
and take this
simple,
one day at a time.

wouldn't
it
be
NICE

to wake up
with no
MORE PAIN.

Pain

eats, eats

away.

so tired

of looking

for

relief

day after day after night.

SHUT TIGHT

in sight
to dream
to sleep
lay my weary body down
an endless chore
to close the bedroom door

stop—cease all
feel as if I'm to fall
tired body awaits
hungry stomach aches

you'd rather have nothing
my virtue and talent
a little angry at that
another man running the show
I'd rather see you home.

my own
I own my own
raindrops running down
like the tears
of greed

lost in some sort of chaos
TV turbulence, argument
behind it all I see money
raindrops run down
my face of greed

such the less
unfortunate
death by disease
tragedy, accident, or insanity

may we all bring a bouquet
to the breakfast table everyday.

THE
A. B. AND ED
SOUL

still surviving

barely

The pain permeates

my legs, my back, and my head.

I live in a deep, dark hole

of depression and tears.

eating away at my soul
the pain
the wait
never seems to happen
to get to a healing point

am I
I am
in the fight alone

and this is the biggest
most difficult ride
I've ever lived

DIE

Yesterday

sometimes
it's all a blur
falling asleep
in the driveway
puts me in a brain daze

go to bed
wake up so hot
wondering what I've got

hoping for a last
not a war blast
peace is what I need
because

    sometimes
    my body
    my soul
        BLEEDS

PAIN—SPINE

what's it like

inside

spine

you toss

and turn me

what's inside

spine?

You've wrecked

my life.

peace of mind
always searching
it was a never ending day
aching head at night
keep my eyes shut tight

cannot show my face
arms crossed in fear
my heart's so empty

You've shut my eyes again

(you know I'm hungry)

The pain you send

isn't worth

the money I spend

but I'll Rush it

Rush me

once more

those gymnast withdrawals

won't
CRAWL

ARC
I can blend her

shaking

EYES of God

it's a mess
I cannot clear
it
UP
is where I'd rather be
everyone
can see
no one's here
but
      GOD

        only

        sees

        the

        goodness.

SATURDAY'S INSANITY

I didn't do this

this craziness

the weekend's pain

drives me insane

A hard life today.

With thanks,

Thus, this concludes this time period.

I feel the sudden painful twitching of piercing pains throughout my spine, penetrating willfully in this body—through each leg. The muscles cringe and the knife stabs then turns—turns, turning and changing this pain to a healing rain.

May this profile be reflected spectacularly like the amazing prisms of color in God's sunlight. A rainbow of life's changes—arthritic changes?

May God move my mountains and flood my life with HIS REIGN.

2001

TAKE

ME

from my pain?

about

to

break.

So tell me
show me
the way
to save my soul
show me

Pain
never been the same
I pretend
to wrap myself in ribbons
act as though all
is all right

What a moon
I
saw
last
night.

GOD

BLESS

MY

SOUL.

Especially now—
I have nowhere to go.

THE
PAIN
THAT
NEVER GOES
AWAY

When it does
It's only temporary

"I'm
feeling
like
a
window"

Looking inside but never in.

With the sting
Of yesteryear

Somebody tell me why
The reason for
A deadened spine
I cry
For yesteryear
And cry
For God to remove
The aches that soothe.

so mixed
as the beaters
swirl

crooked legs
feel their fire
what really happened?

AND

treat me
one day at a time.

The Fire Inside

still burning

ain't gonna stop

for a long while

Coping mechanisms

have disappeared

The guitar and vocals

somehow do not mix

I'd rather dwell

my company

from the NON-DEGENERATE

past life.

OUR

Journeys

are
all

Temporary

Yes
I wish
I could fly.
like a fish
I swim
like a fish

I feel the speed
of life
real life
comfort me inside
difficult to hold on

God's plan
not mine
messy house
keeps me unaware
want to run and hide
from the mess inside

Find

the

Line

Knowing where the drugs must stop.

MY MIRROR

playing guitar
and singing
with an audience
to clap their hands

waking up
running shoes
proper gear
hoping for the day
you will be near

working out the frustration
to hopes and glamour
to write more poetry
All the life from front to back

GOD

Your will
not mine

how much time behind?

so I ache in pain
who knows
God knows
what the living's for

life
beseeches me
may I answer
the call
and remain powerless
over
what road
I will travel
soon.

Since 1994

the pain
I pray
will go away
some sunny day

up all night
I can cry
"it just comes out
yea, comes out"

so please
hear my plea
salvation roots
I want
my snake-skin
cowboy boots.

agitated
another weight
to bear
in God's light
I pray
for that first
pain-free
sunny day.

The Lye

go hide in your closet
resist the beauty of my world
puncture me with ruins of waste
for this is all you taste.

Regurgitate
Spit back at me
Grit your teeth
Deny my pain
Deny your daughter

You bring me here
never in good cheer
Have a seat my friend
for you
have caused my end.

RELEASED

beauty shines
in your life
I know the strife
I've walked the road
before.

May God's grace
release you from your pain
I thank you
for the rain
thank you
for Your rain.

"I NO LONGER DANCE"

Harmony
Seems to become
and grow so fast
always hoping the glory
will last

Through the trials and tears
yea, it's the life of a manic
yea, it's a fun time
in the city

I'll bring my peace
before my knees
at my bed
I need to be led
I need the constant desire
To be a qualified, loveable lady.

THE POETRY OF PAIN, DISILLUSIONMENT

"I NO LONGER DANCE"

fire

always fire

A furnace

burns

throughout my body

wanting me to feel hopeless

the agony

never seems to fade

like my life

I can only write

to you

Suicide child

Your rewards can be great

May the flood open

from the God's golden gate

Release us from pain.

"I NO LONGER DANCE"

dear lord

please

heal my legs

they shake and wobble

now, I'm jumpy

I cannot walk well

it's hell,

but I'm a believer

and I know

You can heal me.

Mirrored

The forms
the doctors
appointments
where did I fail
"what I'm trying to say
heart over mind…"

Time ticks on
To 5:30 AM
As I lie awake
I've come here to stay
I see it
In my eyes.

SLEEP

no appointments kept
I stay awake trying
to figure feelings, crying
over Christina and
singing until I'm hoarse.

Please God show me
what to do with my 12 string.
It's so BEAUTIFUL.

want sound
waves fluctuating
in your ears
leave your fears
behind
in my place
you'll find

YOUR WAY TO HEAVEN

A Poem of Life

the goodness of this life
I've earned and learned
I may possess
I can care
because it's all mine

My heart's been broken
Tears have flooded these eyes
The loss of my daughter
The abandonment of my husband

Now the suffering physical pain
Surprisingly enough
This has the capability
To keep me sane

May my sobriety continue
Unto the end of my bliss
To the life I miss
Across the ocean of mine
I can live until my time
chooses to cease.

The way music
spins me around?
Like an aerial cartwheel,
handspring on the horse,
a truly graceful walk down the beam
that
and
a 50 meter mile swim.
That is what GOD has given back to me.

"I NO LONGER DANCE"

we're not sure
when death comes
something unexplainable
yet we will all
face that mirror

sometime slowly
it hits like a ton of bricks
we suffer
everyday
hoping life will stay

and outward appearances
are not reality at all
that's what I've learned
"without your love
where would I be (right) now"

Legacy of Poets

Think of them
Writing in pen
all day, all night
never giving up on sight
knowing someday
they will die.

leaving behind a legacy
of love to learn
if we take the chance
to romance their dance
words on paper
fill the soul
that's what this life is for
"it's no ordinary world"

Tri-Athlete & More

some keep running
some stop walking
others ache in their legs
ride in a wheelchair
yet my pride
keeps me bound

some swim miles
then run miles beyond
they then have the perseverance
to ride nineteen miles

they stretch every muscle
every muscle unknown
cartwheels turn into aerials
then limbers spring
into back & front
flip—flops
This is me. A world I once knew.

D. D. D.

The pain
no longer concerns me
No pill, it seems, consolidates me
It's a drag
Everyday
Everyday might
especially the mornings
As I lay awake and wonder
How did I arrive at this

    DISEASE

    worsening.

STAINS

on the carpet
in the wall
on the driveway
which way which way
do I turn
when I can't even drive

on my record
lasting forever
just say "YES SIR!"
in my white winter coat
supposed to float
through this
when I can't drive

STAINS DON'T COME OUT

RISK

TAKER

always took

the pain

always took

the blade.

Birthday Blues

made my amends
kept my appointment
I'm a very difficult case
no one wants to put up
with this pitiful face

God give me your grace
I'm on my way to the mailbox
to see what's inside
Probably nada
Birthday blues

no one to stop
and say
I love you.

Only music can take me away.
That and death.

Constant
Except for sleep
Shaking hand
Lead me to my music

D. D. D. does not go away
I feel the pain everyday.

2002

legs
the legs
I used to have
so strong and steady
always ready
to cast anything
beneath the sky
they twirled
and they whirled
hated to wait
to take their turn
always ready
for a muscle burn
NOW?
they wobble
barely can I walk

the pain seethes
throughout every vein
the pain moves
treacherously
through every muscle

my back cries
for relief
it's darkened skull
now the devil's playground
and what can I do
LIE
    down
LIE
    down
LIE
    down
LIE
    down

what a riot
what I scream
eat my heart
soul to die
hear me
you do not
cannot
will not
cry.

pressure of a BIG MAC truck
surges my soul
all I know they say
is let it go
manic depression
kills my dream
so I lie
inside
and scream.

am I here yet?
bloody hands
scrapes and cigarette burns
let me know I'm alive

glory of the night
might heal my spine
it's always on my mind
are we there yet?

You Bet!

SEND

ME

TO YOUR SPIRIT.

SEASONS
OF
DESTRUCTION

I'D RATHER STAY ASLEEP

IT WORKS

peace
after prayer
direction and guidance
like a satellite
like an ocean's flow

blue
crystallized and clear
a carpet ride
into
and sailing
through the endless sky
not asking why
or how
it's all now
present and near.

The tired spine
the legs danced
Beyond eternity
I could see all the time
Coming the crash
of my spine.

Some never and will never
Comprehend the pain
The loss of my legs
The loss of a spirit
So alive, so driven
To God I give
These anguished losses
For no one could
Ever replace
This broken heart.

Struggling with publishing poetry
the need?
is it a need
to give me recognition
successfully happy

I know how excited I would be

Incessant Glorification

be ever so careful
the words upon my lips
the words upon your lips
do they harm
do they give character
and help
an empty place

awards and honors
proudly worn around my neck
yes, the way life was
sound fun.

I dance now in the clouds
see my glitter in the sunlight
hear my moonlight call
and breezes all around

this is my world today.

wounded
in a sheltering fight

flooded
in a sheltering storm

the ties that bind
have let loose unto the tiger

She rests now
from the battlefield
of life.

MRI

to the tomb
you need to go
no time clock
ticking here
see what it's like
feel the enclosure
no movement or sound
you'd scream and holler
your life depends upon the dollar

No one can help you
You're here to say
day after day
don't even sigh
Your life
is a MRI.

A Summons

I give to You
all my cares
my conflicts and confusion
Cast upon You
I give my doubts
all thoughts
containing/pertaining to my friends
my daily way of life
my peace, my strife.

You are always ready to listen
ready to guide me
in the correct direction
I give You my pain
agitation and grief
my tears, my laughter

Most of all dear God
I give my deepest gratitude.

WAIT

weightless hours
flying saucers
lights that blind
what happened to the music

lost in the decay
of a rotten past
erasure cannot be taken
only another road
that must be filled
with hope.

Keep Me Safe

rat in a cage
go around and around
wondering where I'm bound

if only I was normal
no pain, no mania
no depression and tears
there's so much I fear
with so much to lose

and what a price
I hope I don't have to pay.

nightmares
enough to be real
sometimes hard to distinguish
what the truth
will be
please

        NO
        JURY

wait until afternoon
to pick myself up again?

I think I might
(how ambiguous)
lie down.

Oh—and Alice
don't forget to pray.

"if only…"

Don't Even Write the Word

will I always be at odds
until my end
and when will it end
this bed I must sleep in
what a grave and nasty sin

it festers and it grows
from court to court
from tomorrow until the night

please God
may I continue
to keep You in sight
this goes farther and farther
and still there is no end

may I have, somehow
a new beginning
another chance.

Tess' Cure

Baths
Useless hair
Bulging tummy
Fattening legs
Soon,
I will rise above
Because I have cherished
In my heart
God's guidance
God's love

My life demands to gloriously happen.

FAITH, HOPE and LOVE

Waiting and hoping
Loving all those
Who surround me
On my knees
Praying for justice

God, do your work
In this life of mine
I'm running out of time
I pray you keep my lawyer
Walking a solid yellow line.

The Numbers Prove Truths

No needle
No heavy drugs
The pain remains
Physically.

No pillow
No towel
Ugly clothes
Drag on the ground
I'll be damned
If I ever go back there
Again.

After the New Year

What is it
That drives people
in a world
crushed by sin
I'll find my hope
from within

Better days
So easily tossed around
Not knowing the outcome
Keeps me
On my knees.

My music has returned

healing a confused heart

trusting God once again

this I know is true.

Love
Me

for who I am
for who I am

not for what I do.

Meditation for the Day

Persevere in all that God's guidance moves me to do. The persistent carrying out of what seems right and good will bring me to the place where I want to be. If I look back over God's guidance, I will see that His leading has been very gradual and that only as I have carried out His guidance, as far as I can understand, has God been able to give me more clear and definite leading.

I am led by God's guidance on a quick and responsive mind.

PRAYER:

I pray that I may persevere in doing what seems right. I pray that I may carry out all of God's leading, as far as I can understand it all.

Alice Randall Cocca

Meditation for the Day

I believe that God has already seen my heart's needs before I cry out to Him, before I am conscious of those needs myself.

I believe that God is already preparing the answer.

God does not have to be petitioned with sighs and tears and much speaking.

He has already anticipated my every want and need. I will try to see this as these plans unfold in my life.

Alice Randall Cocca

Closing

"Good people are taken away, but no one understands. Those who do right are being taken away from evil and are given peace. Those who live as God wants find rest in death." (Isaiah 57: 1-2)

"The Lord hears good people when they cry out to Him and He saves them from all their troubles." (Psalm 34:17)

"Come to me, all of you who are tired and have heavy loads, and I will give you rest." (Matthew 11:28)

My twin sister died on November 2, 2003 due to complications with degenerative disc disease. After her death, I began to read the many, many journals she had kept over the years. As I read each one, page by page, I realized that she had always wanted to publish her writings but her debilitating disease kept her from doing so. I knew in my heart that my sister wanted me to publish her work. Her poetry was her legacy—her gift to me. As I read her writings, I began to feel the pain she endured. It brought me emotional heartache to read each poem. My heart still cries. Through my sister's unfailing faith in God, she was able "to run with endurance the race that was set before her", (Hebrews 12: 1-2) as she lifted her eyes to heaven.
It gives me peace to know that "God has wiped away every tear"
from my sister's eyes, and she "will have no more sadness, crying, or pain." (Revelation 21:4)

"She rests now from the battlefield of life".

Your Stairway To Heaven

You have left us
On your stairway to heaven
You have reached the top
There will be happiness
No more tears
No more sadness
No more pain
Only joy
Only peace

You have climbed the last step
God has prepared a place for you
You will again begin to dance
Your body has been healed
You can live in perfect form,
Perfect grace, and perfect peace.

You have left us
You have climbed your stairway to heaven.

Marie Randall Chandler

Cartwheels In The Sky

My dear sweet sister
I see your cartwheels in the sky.
You can now run through cool green fields.
You can now jump over whispering streams.

My dear sweet sister
You sing out loud in heavenly choirs.
You play your music with sheer joy.

Your feet can dance a million dances
as you swirl and glide across golden floors.

Your heart is full of happiness
You are of perfect form
Your eyes only see beauty
They no longer hold tears.

My dear sweet sister
I see your cartwheels in the sky.

                                        Marie Randall Chandler

*Once you're born, you start to die. If I knew it wasn't real,
I'd swear it was dream. Make every day count while you're
on Earth, because one day you will just be a memory.
Find the Lord, for only through Him, we'll have everlasting life,
and when you close your eyes on Earth, you will open them
forever to live in grace with Jesus.
May Jesus enter your life and never leave.*
AC

0-595-32483-5

Printed in Great Britain
by Amazon